Comptroller of the Currency
Administrator of National Banks

US Department of the Treasury

A Guide to the National Banking System

A Guide to the
National
Banking System

Washington, DC

April 2008

This guide, prepared by the Office of the Comptroller of the Currency (OCC), is intended to provide an overview of the national banking system, its regulatory structure, and entrance into it. The OCC encourages organizing groups, financial institutions not currently regulated by the OCC, and national banks to consult with appropriate OCC contacts or counsel familiar with banking law to obtain advice on specific issues.

Table of Contents

Introduction

This guidprovides an overview of the national banking system, its regulation, and the Office of the Comptroller of the Currency (OCC). Specifically, it:

- Provides background on the national banking system.

- Provides an overview of the OCC's organization, including its mission, structure, and staff.

- Discusses the value and approach of OCC supervision.

- Outlines the OCC's corporate application process and discusses permissible banking activities for national banks.

- Discusses the OCC's supervision philosophy and its examination process.

- Shows how the OCC uses checks and balances to ensure equitable, quality supervision.

- Includes OCC contacts, additional OCC publications, and other resources.

This page intentionally left blank.

Creation of the National Banking System

The national banking system was conceived by President Abraham Lincoln and Treasury Secretary Salmon P. Chase to revive the national economy and promote a uniform system of currency and credit. The National Currency Act (Act), which created the national banking system, was enacted in 1863. Provisions of that act were reenacted and clarified by the National Bank Act a year later, in 1864. The opening in Philadelphia of the first bank chartered under the new system presented the United States with a fresh means to promote a sense of nationhood based on uniformly regulated financial institutions and a growing economy. The issuance of "national bank notes" by national banks alleviated a serious obstacle to interstate commerce that existed before the Civil War.

Under the direction of the Comptroller of the Currency, the national banking system acquired a reputation for safety and soundness that inspired confidence from the banking public.

The System Today

Today the national banking system consists of around 2,000 national banks, their branches, and other facilities located throughout the United States and in many countries around the world. Although national banks are no longer involved in creating paper currency, they continue to play a critical role in creating and distributing the nation's wealth, to ensure a healthy, growing economy.

The OCC Today

The OCC's mission is to charter national banks, to oversee a nationwide system of banking institutions, and to assure that national banks are safe and sound, competitive and profitable, and capable of serving in the best possible manner the banking needs of their customers. The OCC's mission ensures a robust and financially sound national banking system in which national banks soundly manage their risks, comply with applicable laws, compete effectively with other providers of financial services, offer products and services that meet the needs of customers, and provide fair access to financial services and fair treatment of their customers. For more than 140 years, the OCC has been a leader in examining national banks, evaluating industry trends, identifying emerging banking issues, and, through the supervisory process, assisting national banks to meet the challenges of today's fast-changing financial markets.

Throughout its history, the OCC has sought to provide the highest quality bank supervision. The OCC's approach to bank supervision has evolved in response to the experiences of many years. It is based on a judicious combination of on- and off-site activity conducted by locally based examiners and front-line supervisors who know the communities where national banks operate. It is backed by the strength and depth of a national organization of professionals dedicated to the interests of a safe, sound, fair, and competitive banking system. The OCC maintains a high-quality, professional staff of bank examiners, risk specialists, economists, and attorneys to ensure quality bank supervision.

The OCC also ensures that supervision is fair and balanced. The OCC's Office of the Ombudsman serves a key role in making the OCC more accessible to the banking industry and its customers. The Ombudsman provides bankers with an avenue to discuss problems in confidence, explore options, and seek advice. The OCC's Customer Assistance Group, part of the agency's Office of the Ombudsman, was created to assist consumers in resolving complaints about national banks, offer guidance, and answer questions.

The OCC

The OCC's staff of national bank examiners and other professional and support personnel examine and supervise national banks and federally licensed branches and agencies of foreign banks. Supervision policy and guidance is centralized at the national level to ensure continuity and consistency nationwide. Although this structure is instrumental in setting the OCC's overall direction, the OCC believes that supervision of a national bank occurs most effectively when performed by staff located in or near the bank. This section describes how the OCC uses a flexible structure, deploys its expert staff, and communicates regularly with bankers to ensure effective supervision at the local level as well as nationwide.

Organization

The OCC's organizational structure is designed to promote top-quality bank supervision. The OCC's structure is flexible so that it can adjust its supervision to changes in the industry's structure and activities. Most importantly, decision-making authority is decentralized through examiners, who interact regularly with national banks. Decentralized decision making, coupled with centralized policymaking and a system of checks and balances, provides national banks with the assurance that OCC's supervision is fair, balanced, and expert with respect to their business focus.

Approximately 1,800 OCC bank examiners work from numerous locations around the country and in London. In addition to its national headquarters in Washington, DC, the OCC maintains district and field offices. Although the national headquarters sets policy and direction and oversees bank supervision, supervision of most national banks is coordinated through four district offices, located in New York City, Chicago, Dallas, and Denver, and 48 field offices located in cities throughout the United States.

Assistant deputy comptrollers (ADCs) in field office locations and examiners-in-charge (EICs) in midsize and large banks maintain close local contacts with individual national banks. The OCC's nationwide examiner staff conducts on-site reviews of national banks and provides ongoing supervision of bank operations. Legal and licensing staffs are based at the national headquarters as well as in the four district offices.

The OCC's broad responsibilities and national perspective give the agency unique breadth and depth in understanding the banking industry and its emerging issues and challenges. The OCC's workforce also includes subject matter experts who work with ADCs and midsize and large bank EICs across the country. Collectively, they enable the OCC to deliver quality supervision effectively at the local level.

Lines of Supervision

The OCC has aligned its domestic supervisory operations into two lines of supervision
— community banks and midsize banks, on one hand, and large banks, on the other. The OCC
implemented this structure to enhance consistency, gain efficiency, and serve the diverse national
bank population more effectively.

- Community bank supervision includes community banks involved mostly in
  traditional banking activities. The OCC's district operations are focused on
  the needs of these national banks.

  Midsize bank supervision generally includes companies with national
  bank assets totaling between $8 and $25 billion, either in a single charter
  or aggregated among several charters. Oversight of these more complex
  organizations is centralized under a single deputy comptroller located in
  Washington, DC, to facilitate consistent supervision.

- Large bank supervision includes the largest national banking companies,
  which generally are involved in the most complex activities and operate over
  wide geographic areas. This line of supervision is coordinated through the
  Large Bank Supervision Department headquartered in Washington, DC, and
  is carried out by examination staff assigned to those companies on a full-time
  basis.

Bank Supervision Staff

The ADCs and large bank EICs are front-line supervisors. They monitor the condition of
assigned banks. They also schedule and conduct regular safety and soundness, compliance,
and specialized area examinations. In addition, they maintain an awareness of trends within the
banking industry and the financial services marketplace and deal with a variety of issues that pose
potential risks to the institutions they supervise. The ADCs supervise the majority of national
bank examiners who work from field offices situated strategically throughout the country to best
serve the population of national banks. Large bank EICs and their staff are assigned supervision
of a particular bank.

The OCC uses a "Portfolio Manager Approach" to bank supervision to build examiners' in-depth
knowledge of community banks and their operating environments. Local examiners, who have
substantial authority, perform the direct bank supervision activities. This fosters effective and
consistent communications between examiners and banks, assures continuity in supervisory
matters, and enhances the OCC's responsiveness to bankers' questions and concerns.

The OCC determines the frequency of its examinations (the supervisory cycle) based on the bank's size, complexity, risk profile, and condition. Examiners meet with bank management and the bank's board of directors throughout the supervisory cycle to obtain information or discuss issues. Full-scope examinations normally are conducted either annually or up to every 18 months (12 CFR 4.6), but examination activities may be spread throughout the supervisory cycle. The portfolio manager contacts bank management to:

- Discuss current issues in the bank and in financial trends.

- Follow-up on matters from prior examinations.

- Explore the bank's plans for new products and services, expansion, or other possible changes.

In this way, the OCC helps national bankers explore possible pitfalls in new products and services, flag emerging areas of concern, and address existing problems before they worsen. In addition, portfolio managers can provide information and tools that may help local bankers evaluate their business.

The OCC assigns a dedicated EIC to each midsize bank to develop and implement a supervisory strategy, with assistance from other examiners who also are involved in the supervision of either community or large banks. Having one examiner assigned overall responsibility for continuous supervisory oversight allows for ongoing communication with bank management. This supervisory structure assists the OCC in the prompt identification of supervisory issues in these growing and increasingly complex institutions.

The OCC maintains a resident onsite EIC, supported by a resident core staff of examiners, in each of the largest banks. These examiners, who report directly to a deputy comptroller in Large Bank Supervision, perform ongoing analysis related to the banks' condition, risk profiles, economic factors, and marketplace developments.

Effective Use of Technology

OCC staff uses technology to promote efficient, consistent supervision and effective communication and to resolve issues quickly. Examiners, even in remote locations, can access a wealth of information through computers loaded with current policy guidance and specialized examination and diagnostic tools, and that are connected to network systems. The OCC's extensive resources are available increasingly to other audiences as well as through the OCC's Web site (http://www.occ.treas.gov/).

National BankNet is a system that allows the OCC to communicate with and deliver services via the Internet to the financial institutions it regulates. Available exclusively to national banks, BankNet is a secure extranet site designed to meet bankers' needs and complement OCC regulatory activities. It accommodates a bank's real-time decision making, improves two-way communications between the bank and the OCC, and delivers products and services of value to bankers. National BankNet serves as a primary system for the agency to communicate with national banks in times of national emergency.

National BankNet contains an electronic process, called e-Corp, for completing, signing, and submitting corporate applications. e-Corp features hyperlinks to all laws, regulations, and licensing terms; the ability to save working drafts of applications; complete application checking; and easy on-line signature and submission. e-Corp is part of the OCC's continuing effort to eliminate unnecessary regulatory burden, simplify administrative processes, enhance communications, reduce paperwork, and take full advantage of e-government mandates.

OCC Staff Expertise

Like the banking industry, the OCC adjusts its hiring, training, and deployment of staff to reflect the changing mix and increasing complexity of bank activities. The OCC seeks to anticipate new needs, and it creates programs to enhance employee expertise in specific areas. The OCC employs experts in consumer compliance, information technology, fraud, fiduciary and asset management, as well as attorneys, economists, and staffs with in-depth knowledge in licensing, bank accounting, retail credit, capital markets, community development, risk modeling, and other areas.

The OCC recognizes the value many bankers derive from having seasoned and knowledgeable examiners with diverse experience and specialized skills examining their banks. The OCC regularly modifies and updates its examiner's training curriculum to ensure that examiners have the knowledge, skills, and abilities needed to supervise banks effectively. As a result, OCC examiners have a broad background on which to base their assessment of the condition of national banks.

The average experience level of OCC's examining staff is more than 14 years. Many years of experience on the job gives the typical examiner insight and perspective from observing and analyzing banks of all kinds in different areas and through various economic conditions. This broad knowledge base enhances the advisory function that examiners can provide to bank management and boards of directors.

The OCC's Outreach Program

The OCC supports national banks by being a leading source of regulatory and supervisory information for the financial services industry. In addition to performing regular on-site examinations and periodic supervisory updates, the OCC disseminates information on emerging issues, supervisory concerns, and industry best practices covering a wide range of issues. These programs include instructor-led workshops designed exclusively for community bank directors and telephone seminars aimed at community national banks but available industry-wide through common technology. These high-quality, cost-effective programs have immediate, practical application and focus on critical industry issues and trends.

Moreover, OCC district and field office staff regularly sponsor outreach meetings with bankers and other local financial service industry stakeholders. Agendas organized to meet the specific needs of the local audience typically include examiner presentations and roundtable discussions on timely supervision matters where participants share ideas and offer different perspectives on the issues of the day. Presentations cover such topics as legal and regulatory developments and changes in banking laws, credit underwriting, retail credit, fraud detection and prevention, interest rate risk, economic updates, community development and investments, consumer and Community Reinvestment Act compliance, Bank Secrecy Act, anti-money laundering, audit, and corporate activities.

The OCC's frontline managers are involved in these outreach efforts. District deputy comptrollers, ADCs, and EICs forge strong relationships with a wide range of industry groups, serving as OCC spokespersons at meetings and conferences with bank executives, boards of directors, and officials of other federal, state, and local government agencies. They also meet with public interest groups and other members of the public to discuss matters of mutual interest and to clarify and enhance understanding of OCC policy.

Communications

The OCC is committed to continual, effective communication with national banks. Communication includes formal and informal conversations, meetings, and written policy guidance and examination reports. The OCC strives to be professional, objective, clear, informative, and consistent in all communications. Examiners communicate with bank management and board members as often as the bank's condition and interests and the examiners' findings require.

The OCC periodically provides material to bankers about changes in laws, regulations, and supervisory policy. Issuances also discuss emerging issues, threats to the banking industry, and possible frauds. The OCC disseminates information in advisory letters, alerts, bulletins, handbooks, and manuals. Issuances are available electronically to the industry and general public on the OCC's Web site and through BankNet for national banks.

The *Comptroller's Handbook,* which contains policies and procedures for national bank examinations, is updated regularly. The handbook provides in-depth discussions of the various aspects of bank products and services, including associated risks. Additionally, the handbook (http://www.occ.treas.gov/handbook/chndbk.htm) provides guidance on the OCC's expectations for management and oversight.

The *Comptroller's Licensing Manual* (Licensing Manual) explains OCC policies and procedures for establishing, acquiring, or converting to a national bank, and effecting structural changes and corporate expansion. The Licensing Manual (http://www.occ.treas.gov/corpapps/corpapplic.htm) describes requirements for corporate applications and the processes for public comment and OCC review and analysis of both.

The OCC also disseminates information on "best practices" to strengthen the national banking system. This includes information on various subjects, such as credit underwriting, privacy, and community development.

Assessments and Fees

The OCC is a nonappropriated federal agency funded through assessments and fees paid by national banks. The OCC publishes an assessment and fee schedule at least annually in a bulletin entitled, "Notice of Comptroller of the Currency Fees." A copy of the current schedule may be obtained from the OCC's Communications Division or by visiting our Web site at http://www. occ.treas.gov/.

The National Bank Charter

The national bank charter is a flexible, dynamic license to provide a broad array of financial products and services. This section describes how the OCC's licensing process works, in general, and then focuses on alternative means of entry into the national banking system, such as acquiring a national bank charter. It then describes the broad range of activities available to national banks and how they may be structured.

The OCC's Licensing Process

The Licensing Manual describes requirements for:

- Applications to establish, acquire, or convert to a national bank, and

- Existing national banks to effect corporate changes, including geographical expansion through branching, merger, acquisition, and structural changes to enable delivery of new products or services.

The Licensing Manual sets out OCC's policies and step-by-step procedures, so that applicants know what to do and what to expect from the OCC. The OCC works continually to streamline application filing and review processes and to minimize burden, consistent with maintaining safety and soundness and satisfying statutory requirements. Staff conducts internal reviews and obtains feedback from applicants to spot areas for improvement.

The Licensing Manual is available on the OCC's Web site, including current application forms. The OCC is equipped to accept an ever-increasing volume and variety of application material electronically from national banks through e-Corp on National BankNet.

Licensing and legal staffs in the district offices and national headquarters are available by telephone, e-mail, or meetings, to advise applicants and answer their questions. This is particularly useful for the early discussion of proposals that are unusual or highly complex.

The OCC will accept draft applications and provide feedback to applicants before they file an application. The OCC may approve or conditionally approve or deny any filing after reviewing the application and considering all relevant factors. The OCC may impose conditions if it determines that they are necessary or appropriate to ensure that approval is consistent with applicable statutes, regulations, OCC policies, and safe and sound banking practices.

Entry into the National Banking System

There are two dominant ways that an organizing group, company, or bank can enter the national banking system:

- Establish a new national bank.

- Convert an existing institution to a national bank.

A national bank may be owned directly by individuals or a holding company. The OCC requires each proposed organizer, director, principal shareholder, and executive officer to submit biographical and financial reports in connection with applications for *de novo* charters and certain other types of corporate applications. The OCC conducts background checks to assess a person's competence, experience, integrity, and financial ability, to determine the person's qualification to serve in the proposed capacity. The OCC also may require certain information from a corporate filer along with financial reports. (See the Interagency Biographical and Financial Reports form in the "Background Investigations" booklet of the Licensing Manual.)

Establish a New National Bank

The OCC approves proposals to establish national banks that will foster healthy competition, operate in a safe and sound manner, and have a reasonable chance of success. In so doing, the OCC does not guarantee that a proposal to establish a national bank is without risk to the organizers or investors. The OCC's decision on a proposed new charter depends primarily on its assessment of the organizers' qualifications, choice of management, and strength of their business plan.

Given the importance of strong, new, independent charters and the serious commitment required from an organizing group, the OCC encourages early contact with licensing staff so that organizers can discuss plans and confirm required steps in the chartering process. Once an organizing group is ready to proceed, the OCC will schedule a prefiling meeting, which all organizers must attend.

Throughout the chartering process, the OCC's licensing staff works closely with local examiners who will supervise the new bank. By the time a new bank opens at the end of a successful chartering process, staff from the OCC's supervisory office and the organizers normally will be well acquainted with each other. (See the "Charters" booklet of the Licensing Manual for a complete discussion of the chartering process.)

Convert an Existing Institution to a National Bank

Another alternative for entering the national banking system is to convert a financial institution with a different type of charter. Under applicable statutes and regulations, state banks, state savings banks, and other state banking institutions engaged in the business of receiving deposits, as well as federal savings associations, may convert directly to national bank charters.[1] Conversions generally are not subject to a public notice and comment period. The OCC has an expedited process for converting institutions that have favorable ratings from their current regulators and a sound capital structure. A detailed discussion of conversion transactions is contained in the "Conversions" booklet of the Licensing Manual.

Permissible National Bank Activities

National banks may engage in activities that are part of, or incidental to, the business of banking, or are otherwise authorized for a national bank. The OCC publishes *Activities Permissible for a National Bank,* available on the OCC's Web site. The business of banking is an evolving concept, and the permissible activities of national banks similarly change over time. Accordingly, this list contained in the publication is not exclusive; the OCC may permit national banks to conduct additional activities in the future. Any activity described in the publication's summary as permissible for a national bank also is permissible for an operating subsidiary of a national bank.

The national bank charter permits several options for corporate structure. This gives national banks flexibility to structure their operations in whatever way is most advantageous for them. Applications by national banks for changes to enable them to engage in new activities may be subject to the OCC's licensing process, as described earlier. OCC licensing and legal experts are available for consultation and advice. Examiners from the bank's local supervisory office, or specialists elsewhere in OCC, can help evaluate any supervisory implications of new proposals.

A national bank does not need OCC approval to perform any bank-permissible activity directly in the bank. Banks may alternatively perform activities through other structures, including:

- An operating subsidiary.

- A financial subsidiary.

- A bank service company.

- Other equity investment.

---

[1] Indirect conversions also could occur through merging an interim national bank with the state-chartered entity or federal savings association. For a discussion of mergers involving interim banks, see the "Business Combinations" booklet of the Licensing Manual.

Following are brief descriptions of these alternatives.

Operating Subsidiary

An operating subsidiary is a means through which national banks are authorized to conduct their business. It can be a corporation, limited liability company (LLC), or similar entity. It must be controlled by the national bank, and it may conduct any activity that the parent bank could engage in directly, either as part of, or incidental to, the business of banking, as determined by the OCC or other statutory authority. Although prior OCC approval is required in some cases, simple after-the-fact notice to the OCC may be sufficient in other cases. For further information on operating subsidiaries, see OCC regulations at 12 CFR 5.34 and the "Investment in Subsidiaries and Equities" booklet of the Licensing Manual.

Financial Subsidiary

As authorized by the Gramm-Leach-Bliley Act, a financial subsidiary is a corporation, LLC, or similar entity, controlled by one or more insured depository institutions, that conducts activities that are "financial in nature" or incidental to financial activities. Financial subsidiaries do not include operating subsidiaries or bank service companies. However, a financial subsidiary may perform activities permissible for national banks to engage in directly in conjunction with activities that are financial in nature or incidental to financial activities. For a bank to own a financial subsidiary, the bank and the subsidiary must meet certain requirements and comply with safeguards. For further information on financial subsidiaries, see OCC regulations at 12 CFR 5.39 and the "Investment in Subsidiaries and Equities" booklet of the Licensing Manual.

Bank Service Company

National banks also may make investments in bank service companies. A bank service company is a corporation, whose capital stock is owned by one or more insured banks, or a LLC, whose members are insured banks. National banks are specifically authorized to control this type of subsidiary by the express terms of a federal statute. Bank service companies may conduct only activities a bank could perform directly, unless the Federal Reserve authorizes them to conduct other activities permissible for bank holding companies. If the bank service company has national and state bank shareholders or members, the activities conducted must be permissible for all of the insured banks. For further information, see the Bank Service Company Act, 12 USC 1861-1867, OCC regulations at 12 CFR 5.35, and the "Investment in Subsidiaries and Equities" booklet of the Licensing Manual.

Other Equity Investment

A national bank and its operating subsidiary may make a noncontrolling investment, or hold a minority interest, in certain enterprises. The OCC regulation (12 CFR 5.36) provides for an after-the-fact notice process if the enterprise is engaged in an activity permissible for after-the-fact notice under the OCC's operating subsidiary regulation (12 CFR 5.34) or if the activity is substantively the same as that contained in published OCC precedent on noncontrolling investments.

Other investors in the business may be other banks or nonbank companies. Minority investments may be used as a way to limit costs, or to enable a bank to engage in a line of business with partners possessing particular experience or other important attributes. This option, therefore, provides national banks with significant business flexibility. For further information, see OCC regulations at 12 CFR 5.36 and the "Investment in Subsidiaries and Equities" booklet of the Licensing Manual.

This page intentionally left blank.

Supervision and Oversight

Overview

The OCC strives to deliver to all national banks the highest possible quality of bank supervision. Supervisory efforts are directed toward identifying material problems, or emerging problems, in individual banks or the banking system, and toward ensuring that such problems are corrected appropriately. Because banking is essentially a business of managing risk, supervision is centered on the accurate evaluation and management of risks. The OCC believes that bankers, and not regulators, should manage their banks. As a result, the OCC expects banks to establish and follow appropriate risk management practices.

The OCC uses an integrated risk-based approach to supervision. The goal of this approach is to maximize the effectiveness of the OCC's supervision process by assessing all bank activities under one supervisory plan. With this integrated approach, each supervisory office ADC or large bank EIC has responsibility for all supervisory activities, including safety and soundness, information technology, asset management, and compliance. Integrating all examining areas under one supervisor ensures that the OCC assesses risks in all areas using the same criteria and that the most significant risks to the bank will receive the most supervisory attention.

Clear and meaningful communication between the OCC and the banks it supervises is a vital component of high-quality supervision. To that end, the OCC publishes on its Web site examination procedures and guidance about evolving issues so that bankers are apprised of OCC examination and supervision activities.

Supervision by Risk

Examiners meet with bank management and the bank's board of directors throughout the supervisory cycle to obtain information or discuss issues. At the completion of the cycle, the examiners prepare a report and conduct a meeting with the bank's board of directors to discuss the results. Those meetings allow participants to discuss the objectives of the OCC's supervision; strategic issues that may be confronting the bank; any major concerns, risks, or issues that may need to be addressed; and other matters of mutual interest.

An environment in which examiners and board members communicate openly and honestly benefits a bank. OCC examiners and professional staff have experience with a broad range of banking activities and can provide independent, objective information on safe and sound banking principles and compliance with laws and regulations.

Risk Assessments

The OCC's primary supervisory objective is to assess each bank's ability to identify, measure, monitor, and control risks through its risk management systems. The OCC does this through its risk assessment process. The OCC has defined nine categories of risk for bank supervisory purposes. Those risks are credit, interest rate, liquidity, price, foreign currency translation, transaction, compliance, strategic, and reputation.

From a supervisory perspective, risk is the potential that events, expected or unanticipated, may have an adverse impact on the bank's earnings and capital. The simple existence of risk is not necessarily reason for concern. To put risks in perspective, the OCC determines whether the risks a bank plans to undertake are warranted. Generally, risks are warranted when they are understandable, measurable, controllable, and within the bank's capacity to readily withstand adverse performance.

Examiners assess the quantity of risk and the quality of risk management. They then assign each risk an aggregate assessment (low, medium, or high) and determine whether the risk is expected to decrease, increase, or remain stable over the next 12 months.

Ratings

Additionally, all financial institutions are evaluated and rated under the Federal Financial Institutions Examination Council's (FFIEC) Uniform Financial Institutions Rating System. This system, which is referred to as the CAMELS rating, assesses six components of a bank's performance: Capital adequacy, Asset quality, Management administration, Earnings, Liquidity, and Sensitivity to market risk. Each component is rated on a scale of 1 to 5, with 1 being the most favorable rating.

A composite or overall rating ranging from 1 to 5 also is assigned under the CAMELS rating system. A rating of "1" indicates the strongest performance and risk management practices relative to the institution's size, complexity, and risk profile. Those institutions present the least level of supervisory concern. Conversely, a 5-rated institution demonstrates critically deficient performance, inadequate risk management practices, and the highest level of supervisory concern.

Specialized Area Supervision

The OCC also reviews specialized functions and areas not specifically addressed in the CAMELS ratings. This includes the Community Reinvestment Act, USA PATRIOT Act (amended the Bank Secrecy Act), consumer compliance, information technology, and asset management. These supervisory programs are risk based and generally integrated into the CAMELS reviews. Examiners with greater knowledge of specialized areas typically conduct the reviews of areas and activities that are deemed high-risk.

For example, the OCC employs compliance specialists who conduct compliance examination work. These compliance specialists report to an ADC or a large bank EIC. In a small bank, generalists usually lead the examination and may be assisted by other generalists, compliance specialists, and other specialty (information technology and asset management) examiners. In a large bank, a compliance specialist generally will lead the compliance examination, assisted by other compliance specialists, generalists, and specialty examiners.

This page intentionally left blank.

Checks and Balances

The OCC builds checks and balances into its high-quality bank supervision program through a number of offices, including the offices of the Ombudsman and Program and Management Accountability.

The Ombudsman

The Office of the Ombudsman is a distinct division of the OCC that operates independently of the agency's bank supervision function. The three primary functions of the Ombudsman's office are: the National Bank Appeals Process, the Bank Examination Questionnaire, and the Customer Assistance Group (CAG). These units share a common goal: to act as catalysts for improvement in the industry and the agency. The Office of the Ombudsman is committed to the core principles of timely and fair dispute resolution and quality customer service.

National Bank Appeals Process

The Office of the Ombudsman administers a national bank appeals process. Established in 1993 and modified in 2002, this process ensures that national banks receive a fair and expeditious review of OCC decisions and actions. The Ombudsman functions independently, outside of the bank supervision and examination area, and reports directly to the Comptroller. With the consent of the Comptroller, the Ombudsman may supersede any OCC decision or action during the resolution of an appealable matter.

Bank Examination Questionnaire

The OCC solicits and receives feedback routinely from the banking industry through "examination questionnaires" and "satisfaction surveys" that accompany reports of examination and decisions on corporate applications, respectively. The OCC uses these tools to gather candid and timely feedback from bankers and others. Bankers' feedback enables OCC management to evaluate the overall effectiveness of supervision and licensing processes and to refine and make improvements continuously. These measurement tools may be completed and submitted electronically through National BankNet.

Customer Assistance Group

The Customer Assistance Group (CAG) acts as a liaison between national banks and their customers. CAG's assistance with customer problem resolution reflects OCC's commitment to ensure fair access to financial services and fair treatment for all national bank customers. CAG provides complaint trends and consumer issues through detailed reports, onsite meetings with bankers, and direct consultation with OCC's supervision staff. Information identified from the complaints can serve as an early warning system that alerts the bank and the OCC to potential areas of risk.

A recent enhancement to CAG services has been the development of CAGNet. This is a Web-based "business-to-business" application that facilitates the paperless transfer of consumer complaints, the banks' responses, and analytical reports via a secure and dedicated extranet application. In addition to improving complaint resolution time, CAGNet has decreased the burden on the industry. To date, CAGNet is available to national banks and may be accessed exclusively through National BankNet.

Program and Management Accountability

The OCC's Program and Management Accountability (PMA) units, composed of the Quality Management Division and the Program Analysis Unit, report directly to the Comptroller through the Comptroller's Chief of Staff. The PMA units administer the OCC's internal audit, internal review, program analysis, and also serve as liaison to other audit and investigative offices.

The Quality Management Division oversees enterprise risk management issues, promotes performance excellence initiatives, and manages the liaison function. The Program Analysis Unit provides sophisticated analytical support in the areas of program analysis, budget review, and staffing plans. These units work together to ensure that: 1) the OCC's programs are achieving intended results, 2) resource usage is aligned with the agency's mission, 3) resources are protected from waste, fraud, and abuse, 4) applicable laws and regulations are followed, and 5) reliable and timely management information systems support decision-making.

Appendix A: OCC Locations

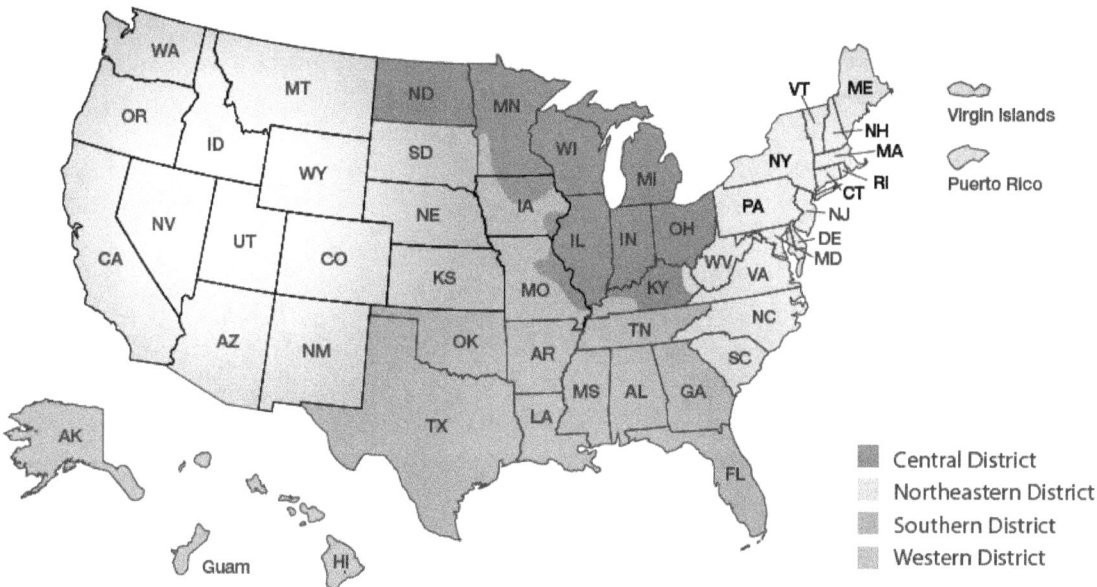

The following pages list headquarters divisions that are referenced in this guide and telephone numbers for district offices. For a complete directory of OCC offices, consult the OCC Web site at http://www.occ.treas.gov/.

Appendix B: OCC Contacts

General Information

Office of the Comptroller of the Currency
250 E Street, SW
Washington, DC 20219-0001

Telephone   (202) 874-5000
Web site   http://www.occ.treas.gov

Selected Headquarters Divisions

Chief Counsel

Telephone   (202) 874-5200
Fax Number   (202) 874-5374

Provides legal advice on a broad range of banking law questions, federal securities laws, electronic banking, consumer protection laws, corporate structure and governance, lending limits, affiliate insider transactions, international banking, among other banking matters.

Chief National Bank Examiner

Telephone   (202) 874-2870
Fax Number   (202) 874-5352

Has responsibility for formulating and disseminating the OCC's supervision policies to promote national bank safety and soundness and compliance with laws and regulations. The department issues policy, guidance, and examination procedures related to national banks' commercial, consumer, asset management, capital markets, and community compliance activities.

Communications

Telephone   (202) 874-4700
Publications   (202) 874-4884
Fax Number   (202) 874-5263

Provides information, publications, and design services for the OCC. It also operates and oversees the Public Information Room, which offers access to OCC public documents; and processes initial requests filed under the Freedom of Information and Privacy Acts.

Community Affairs

Telephone	(202) 874-5556
Fax Number	(202) 874-4652

Helps national banks to provide community development financing and retail services to underserved consumers and communities. Staff, located in headquarters and the districts, provide assistance on local community development resources; sponsor forums for exchanging ideas among lenders, community groups, and government officials; conduct research and develop publications on best practices; and administer the OCC's Part 24 Community Development Investment Authority.

Community Bank Activities

Telephone	(202) 874-4861
Fax Number	(202) 874-5305

Coordinates the OCC's efforts to reduce burden and assist in making supervision more effective and helpful for community banks.

Compliance

Telephone	(202) 874-4428
Fax Number	(202) 874-5221

Has responsibility for the development of compliance policy and examination procedures and liaison with compliance experts in the field and with other agencies.

Customer Assistance Group (CAG)

Comptroller of the Currency
1301 McKinney, Suite 3450
Houston, Texas 77010

Toll-free Number	(800) 613-6743
Fax Number	(713) 336-4301

E-mail	Customer.assistance@occ.treas.gov

Acts as a liaison between national banks and their customers but is not an advocate for either party. CAG provides assistance with problem resolution. It also evaluates complaint trends and consumer issues, serving as an early warning system for potential areas of risk.

International Banking and Finance

Telephone	(202) 874-4730
Fax Number	(202) 874-5234

Has responsibility for maintaining relations and information exchange with foreign supervisors, coordinating OCC participation in the FBO Supervision Program in support of the supervision of federal branches and agencies, and assessing potential risks associated with banks' cross-border exposures.

Large Bank Supervision

Telephone	(202) 874-4610
Fax Number	(202) 927-0631

Has responsibility for supervision of the largest national banking companies that generally are involved in more complex activities and operate over wide geographic areas.

Licensing

Telephone	(202) 874-5060
Fax Number	(202) 874-5293
Web site	bos@occ.treas.gov

Has responsibility for developing and applying OCC licensing policy. It provides support and guidance to the district licensing staffs in their processing of applications filed in the districts.

Midsize Bank Supervision

Telephone	(202) 874-0685
Fax Number	(202) 874-5339

Has responsibility for supervision of midsize national banking companies and credit card banks that generally are involved in more complex activities than community banks and operate over wide geographic areas.

Ombudsman

Comptroller of the Currency
1301 McKinney Street, Suite 3400
Houston, Texas 77010

Telephone	(713) 336-4350
Fax Number	(713) 336-4351

Has responsibility for overseeing the national bank appeals process and the customer assistance group.

OCC District Offices

Northeastern

1114 Avenue of the Americas	(212) 819-9860
Suite 3900	Fax (212) 790-4098
New York, NY 10036-7780	
Deputy Comptroller	(212) 790-4001
District Counsel	(212) 790-4010
Licensing Manager	(212) 790-4055

Supervises most national banks headquartered in Connecticut, Delaware, District of Columbia, Maine, Maryland, Massachusetts, New Hampshire, New Jersey, New York, North Carolina, Pennsylvania, Puerto Rico, Rhode Island, South Carolina, Vermont, Virginia, the Virgin Islands, and West Virginia. Generally, field or local satellite offices also are located in these states.

Southern

500 North Akard Street, Suite 1600	(214) 720-0656
Dallas, Texas 75201-3394	Fax (214) 720-7000
Deputy Comptroller	(214) 720-7005
District Counsel	(214) 720-7012
Licensing Manager	(214) 720-7052

Supervises most national banks headquartered in Alabama, Arkansas, Florida, Georgia, Louisiana, Mississippi, Oklahoma, Tennessee, and Texas. Generally, field or local satellite offices also are located in these states.

Central

One Financial Place, Suite 2700   (312) 360-8800
440 South LaSalle Street   Fax (312) 435-0951
Chicago, Illinois 60605-1073

Deputy Comptroller   (312) 360-8802

District Counsel   (312) 360-8805

Licensing Manager   (312) 360-8851

Supervises most national banks headquartered in Illinois, Indiana, Kentucky, Michigan, Minnesota, Missouri, North Dakota, Ohio, South Dakota, and Wisconsin. Generally, field or local satellite offices also are located in these states.

Western

1225 17th Street, Suite 300   (720) 475-7600
Denver, Colorado 80202   Fax (720) 475-7690

Deputy Comptroller   (720) 475-7603

District Counsel   (720) 475-7630

Licensing Manager   (720) 475-7650

Supervises most national banks headquartered in Alaska, Arizona, California, Colorado, Guam, Hawaii, Idaho, Iowa, Kansas, Missouri, Montana, Nebraska, Nevada, New Mexico, Northern Mariana Islands, Oregon, Washington, Wyoming, and Utah. Generally, field or local satellite offices also are located in these states.

Appendix C: OCC Publications

OCC publications that you may find useful are listed in this appendix. To request an order form and a list of publications, contact the OCC's Communications Division at (202) 874-4700. Electronic copies of these and other OCC publications are available in a downloadable and searchable format on the OCC's Web site at http://www.occ.treas.gov/.

Comptroller's Licensing Manual

The Licensing Manual consists of a series of booklets. The booklets explain the OCC policies and procedures to form a new national bank, for existing institutions to enter the national banking system, for individuals to acquire control of a national bank, and for national banks to effect structural changes and expand activities.

Comptroller's Handbook

This handbook consists of a series of booklets on fundamental topics of bank supervision. The Community Bank Supervision and Large Bank Supervision Handbooks explain the OCC's supervisory approaches for these two lines of business and contain standards and procedures that guide examiners in reaching conclusions about a bank's operations. Other booklets provide more detailed descriptions and examination procedures for areas.

Comptroller's Handbook for Asset Management

This publication consists of several booklets that present policies and procedures for the examination of the asset management activities of national banks.

Comptroller's Handbook for Compliance

The booklets comprising this publication contain the procedures used in examining national banks for compliance. The handbook is a supervisory tool for examiners performing compliance examinations and a self-assessment tool for bankers analyzing bank compliance systems.

Selected Other OCC Publications

Activities Permissible for a National Bank. This report describes the activities that are authorized for a national bank as part of, or incidental to, the business of banking.

The OCC Annual Report. This report sets forth the agency's accomplishments in supervision, regulation, risk analysis, and chartering. It also describes management initiatives, financial management results, and OCC outreach to industry, community, and consumer organizations.

Detecting Red Flags in Board Reports – A Guide for Directors, Comptroller of the Currency, October 2003. This booklet describes information generally found in board reports that national bank directors use to meet their fiduciary responsibility. It highlights red flags that may signal existing or potential problems.

The Director's Book: The Role of the National Bank Director, Comptroller of the Currency, March 1997. This publication provides general guidance to directors of national banks.

Interpretations and Actions. This publication is published monthly and has been available on the OCC's Web site since May 1996. It includes legal staff interpretations, trust interpretative letters, securities letters, and bank accounting advisory series, which represent the informal views of the Comptroller's staff concerning the applications of banking law to contemplated activities or transactions.

National Banks and the Dual Banking System, Comptroller of the Currency, September 2003. This paper explains the history and features of the "dual banking system" and discusses the judicial and legislative precedents establishing the constitutional limits on the ability of states to control or direct national bank powers conferred under federal law.

Quarterly Journal. This publication is published in March, June, September, and December and has been available on the OCC's Web site since 1997. It is the journal of record for the most significant actions and policies of the OCC. It is published only in electronic form four times a year.

Report of the Ombudsman, Comptroller of the Currency, December 2002. It includes descriptions of the appeals process, the Customer Assistance Group, and the results of the examination questionnaires.

www.ingramcontent.com/pod-product-compliance
Lightning Source LLC
Chambersburg PA
CBHW080639290526
45790CB00007B/3137